T0194046

George Givens

The
Hired Man's Christmas

SCRIBNER

SCRIBNER
1230 Avenue of the Americas
New York, NY 10020

Previously published by Parley Street Publishing
First Scribner edition 1998
SCRIBNER and design are trademarks of
Simon & Schuster Inc.

Designed by Brooke Zimmer
Set in Sabon Monotype
Manufactured in the United States of America

1 3 5 7 9 10 8 6 4 2

Library of Congress Cataloging-in-Publication Data
Givens, George W., 1932–
The hired man's Christmas / George Givens.
        p.   cm.
        I. Title.
    PS3557.I848H57   1998
    813'.54—dc21   98-29784
            CIP

ISBN 978-1-9821-0226-5

To our children—
Chip, Sandy, Terryl, Danny,
Ginny, Bobbie, Sean, and Sarah—
and for the love they bring back to
our home each time they return

Acknowledgments

Thanks to my daughters for their help:
Bobbie for editing
and
Ginny for interior illustrations.

Contents

The Hired Man's Christmas

I

Frank

HIS PITIFULLY FEW BELONGINGS HE CARRIED in a traditional hobo bag tied to the end of a stick over his shoulder. The day wasn't yet as hot as upstate New York summers can be—it was still midmorning on that July day—but the beads of sweat were already gathered on his weathered forehead under the brim of his soiled straw hat. The early-morning chores were finished, breakfast was out of the way, and another hard day of haying was beginning on my grandfather's farm.

My dad was heading for the fields with a team and dump rake to rake yesterday's cutting into windrows for the hay-loader. My two brothers, Duane and Roger, were helping my grandfather hitch up another team to begin hauling the first load of hay for the day. Louie and I were already on the wagon, waiting for a ride to the hayfield, where we would then get off and follow the wagon while it was being loaded. Because I was several years younger than my brothers, my parents had taken in Louie, a foster child two years older than I was. I never did figure out whether it was felt I needed someone close to my age as I was growing up on our isolated hilltop farm, or whether it was to have two more farmhands to take the place of my older brothers when they left home.

Whatever the case, Louie came to live with us when I was five years old and stayed until I was fourteen. Because my two brothers were so much older than I, Louie became, in essence, my "brother" and childhood companion for nine memorable years. We did all those things together and shared the same childhood experiences that brothers normally share. Louie, as I recall, had arrived at our home only a year before the story begins.

Our visitor, who had apparently been walking some distance that morning on the dirt road that passed our Gee Hill farm, shuffled up the driveway toward us. My granddad—Bah, our family called him—glanced up as our unusual visitor timidly approached him, ignoring us kids. Of course, in the 1930s children were "to be seen and not heard" anyway, especially if those children were a six-year-old like me or an eight-year-old like Louie, so we made no attempt to greet him either. But hobos on Gee Hill were too much of a rarity for us to ignore, so we listened closely to hear how Bah would reject his request for a handout. A hardscrabble clay-hill farm during the Depression offered mighty slim pickings for seekers of charity. As it turned out, the old man wasn't asking for charity. He wanted a job. Even at my early age I knew my granddad couldn't afford to pay a hired man, so I wasn't at all surprised when Bah, in his gentle but firm manner, told the stranger that as much as we needed help, he just couldn't afford to hire anyone.

"I ain't looking for pay," the hobo replied, "just a place to sleep and some food for my belly." Bah pondered this for a moment before speaking. "Well, let's check with the boss," he said, then led the way to the kitchen to consult with my grandmother.

Apparently Grandma Ora was amenable to the idea—she always did have a soft spot for "down-and-outers"—because a few minutes later Bah returned from the house alone. In response to our quizzical looks, he explained, "As soon as he gets a bite of breakfast, he'll be out to give us a hand."

Thus began our annual summer association with Frank, the "hired man." It was obvious that Frank was used to hard work. He never had to be asked to do a particular task, and not only did he know exactly what needed doing, he always did it well. My grandfather, I sensed, was embarrassed at not being able to pay wages to such a valuable farmhand, but Frank didn't seem to have any material needs. He turned down invitations to go into town with my grandparents and appeared uneasy when there was not plenty of work to keep him occupied.

My grandmother gave him the little room at the top of the stairs and he ate his meals with the family, but he still remained pretty much a loner. He spent most of his spare time by himself just thinking, or at least steering clear of any personal involvement with our family.

Only one time can I recall him getting involved. It happened early one morning as we were getting ready for the day's work. My dad was hitching one of the teams to the mowing machine when my granddad came out of the barn.

"Morris, what are you doing?" he asked.

Without even looking in his direction, my dad replied matter-of-factly, "Going to do some more mowing."

"Don't you think we have enough down already? Put much more down and it'll get wet before we can haul it."

Turning toward his father and scowling, Dad snapped, "Know something about the weather the rest of us don't?"

My grandfather would only have countered with a gentle response if at all, but Frank hadn't yet gotten to know Bah well enough to know that about him. He was suddenly at my grandfather's side, grabbing his arm and pulling him toward the open door of the barn from which he had just emerged. "Let Morris do his work; we'll do ours . . . perhaps a little faster in case that rain comes," he added with a slight smile.

My dad and his father seldom ever disagreed. Bah seldom disagreed with anyone. And even had Frank not gotten involved, this incident would probably have blown over quickly and been forgotten. It was obvious even to Louie and me that Frank had a strong aversion to squabbles, so after that we were all a bit more cautious not to give even the appearance of any wrangling. Apparently, Frank's dislike of discord was even stronger than his craving for the solitude of his private thoughts.

Even during the noon hour, when we all gathered on the front lawn, resting up for the hard afternoon ahead of us, Frank would move away by himself. Knowing he wanted it that way, none of us bothered him until it was time to head for the fields. Then, without hesitation, he would get back to his feet as though he couldn't wait to get back to work and have some activity to occupy his mind.

I wasn't at my grandparents' all of the time; it only seemed that way. My dad's farm was about a mile away, but we worked the two farms together in the summer when heavy labor was most needed. My grandparents had two foster teenage boys, so the workload was fairly evened out. But Frank sure made haying and grain harvesting a lot easier since he never hesitated to take the hardest or dirtiest jobs. During the burning midsummer haying days, this sort of work meant loading the loose hay as it spilled in a steady stream from the hay-loader attached to the back of the wagon, and then later mowing the hay away in the hot hayloft when it was dumped from the horse fork on the overhead track. And during the grain harvest that followed, Frank seemed to run with the heavy grain sacks from the threshing machine outside the barn door to the granary in the barn.

Frank was fairly close to Bah in age—probably around sixty—but to my knowledge he never revealed any of his life history, even to my grandfather. And to the rest of us he was a total mystery.

That mystery deepened one rainy day. It was the kind of day I looked forward to on the farm, and I suppose, even though they complained about what the rain was doing to the cut hay and about the lost time, my dad and granddad were also secretly happy to have the day off. I remember spending such days playing in the hay-mow tunnels created when the hay settled under the barn beams, or exploring the ancient family relics in my grandparents' attic while the comforting sound of the rain drummed on the wooden shingles overhead. If I was home, I might spend a pleasant afternoon lying across my bed near the window reading a Zane Grey novel and listening to the raindrops as they rattled on the leaves of the poplar tree in my father's rose garden.

On that particular day, however, I was at my grandparents' when the rain started. Disappointed because Frank paid so little attention to me, I decided to try to talk to him. I remember climbing to his little bedroom at the top of the stairs. As I looked in at the open door, Frank was sitting on the bed staring out the window that overlooked the valley south of the farm. With a quick glance, he barely acknowledged my presence, and when I softly asked, "What are you doing?" he didn't respond. Even in my youthful mind, I felt I was intruding on some kind of personal sadness. I left him alone and never again went back.

After that, I began to accept Frank's detachment and stopped trying to get his attention. Then one evening at Virgil Creek, I saw another side of Frank, and his character became even more of a puzzle—a puzzle I was unable to solve until years later.

Haying was a hot, dirty job, and after a full day of loading hay or mowing it away in the barn, we were all in need of a refreshing shower. Since we had no running water in either our house or my granddad's, and the stock pond was rather uninviting, we would often finish up our evening chores and pile into Bah's Model A for a four- or five-mile trip to Virgil Creek and a refreshing dip in its clear, cool waters. Even Frank, in his reserved and uncommunicative manner, would join in on this end-of-day ritual.

On this particular summer evening, when I was

about seven years old, we stopped at our usual swimming hole, but after a few minutes of typical horseplay, Louie and I decided to explore farther up the creek. I was in the lead, and we had just gone around a bend when I stepped off into some water well over my head—a somewhat unusual depth in that part of Virgil Creek. Not knowing how to swim, I panicked. My life didn't flash before my eyes, but other thoughts did: "Why did I have to explore this part of the creek?" and "Why doesn't Louie help me?" and "Is this what it's like to die?" Suddenly I felt Louie's arm and grabbed it, shoving myself toward shore and firm ground. As I collapsed on the edge of the bank, I could hear Louie yelling for help. My dad and Frank got to me at about the same time. I vaguely remember my dad scolding me for leaving the rest of the family. I remember Frank's reaction well, however, as it was so out of character for him. He turned on my father angrily: "Doesn't he know how to swim?" After getting a negative answer, Frank lectured my father: "How can you let him get to this age and not have taught him? He almost drowned!"

Uncharacteristically also, my dad didn't respond. And Frank, seemingly embarrassed over his outburst, turned and walked away. The next day Dad took me to the stock pond and taught me to swim. When I mentioned it to Frank, his response was merely a curt "About time."

When the harvest season was over in the fall, Frank would gather together his few necessities and with only a brief "Be seeing you" trudge across the lawn and disappear around Bah's woodshop, down the dirt road.

But each following year, right on schedule, as we were preparing the haying equipment for another season, Frank would reappear, acting as though he had been gone no more than a night or two instead of the nine months it had actually been. I imagine he just took it for granted that there'd be a place at the table and a bed in the little room at the top of the stairs waiting for him.

I don't know that my dad or mother would have accepted Frank as readily as my dad's folks did. Of course, our farm was quite a bit smaller, as was our home. But even if we'd had the room to house a stranger, my dad was not as easygoing as was Bah, and my mother didn't take to "outsiders" as readily as did Grandma Ora. Such contrasting attitudes toward people accounted for my becoming so close to my grandparents at such an early age. In the years that followed, it became increasingly difficult to have the rapport with my father that I shared with Bah. As I look back, the lack of communication between my dad and me stemmed even more largely from his quick and violent temper. This was a great source of conflict between him and my brothers, especially Duane, the oldest, who had a similar temperament. Although my father's outbursts did not normally result in physical punishments, there was always that possibility. When I was no more than eight, my dad had a physical confrontation with Duane, who was then seventeen. This time Duane struck my father back, and a short time later left home for good.

Afraid of similar confrontations as I got older, I used a different tactic. I simply learned to avoid my dad—as much as it was possible while working together on a small farm—hoping that something would change our relationship for the better.

Dad's outbursts seemed to be something he couldn't control, and he undoubtedly regretted them later. But he could neither apologize nor balance his harsh behavior with any displays of affection toward his children. Adding to the problem, undoubtedly, were the harsh circumstances under which we lived on a small, unprogressive farm during the Depression.

Bad luck seemed to hound my father all of his life. Soon after his marriage he found a job as a rural mail carrier—a fairly prestigious occupation for those times. Unfortunately, he resigned to work the farm that we lived on. It was a poor farm and a poor decision, which he realized too late. He decided to supplement his inadequate farm income by buying a truck and carrying the milk from neighboring farms to the milk plant. He soon wrecked the truck and broke his shoulder, losing his entire investment. He slowly built a small herd of milk cows, only to have them come down with brucellosis, a serious infectious disease. The government, offering no compensation, ordered the entire herd destroyed. At that point he was forced to find work in a wire factory ten miles away—a hard, dirty job that probably finished destroying a spirit that would have been an easy-going, kindlier father. Dad could otherwise be charming to friends and neighbors, but we children must have served as a constant reminder of his inability to provide a better living for us.

Only now as a parent can I imagine his feelings on our twice-a-month trip to the Cobakco in Cortland. Food was not easy to come by for millions of families during the Depression, and it certainly wasn't for us. I can remember many evening meals of only cornmeal mush or applesauce, and thinking it normal for any family. Knowing you were not alone in your poverty, however, was not much consolation to a proud man, and my dad, whatever his faults may have been, was honest and proud.

But a family cannot survive solely on pride and cornmeal mush, and every other week, when time permitted, my parents, with Louie and me in the backseat, would drive into Cortland for a few necessities—one of them being bread. My mother was not a bread maker like Grandma Ora was, and she certainly wouldn't have had the time since she often worked outdoors whenever my dad needed an extra hand in driving horses or feeding the livestock. Besides, Cobakco provided us with bread cheaper than it would have cost us to make it. That side trip to the large factory-like bakery was, to me, the highlight of our trips to town. As we approached the large brick building, the delightful odors were overpowering, as was the anticipation of the trip inside. Louie and I were allowed to accompany Dad as long as we made no comments about the purchase.

Up a short flight of stairs was a window counter on the first landing. In response to "What'll it be?" from the man behind the counter, my dad, laying a dime on the counter, always said, "A box of dog food."

To my youthful eyes the box seemed huge and was filled with the most unimaginable eatables. My dad knew that the box contained broken pieces of sugar doughnuts, half-moon cookies, and sliced bread that had only recently, perhaps, been picked off the floor of the bakery and thrown into the "dog food" boxes to be sold to poor farmers like my dad. With the box sitting between Louie and me on the backseat, the temptation was irresistible and I was always amazed that my parents never caught us sneaking tastes of those delightful tidbits. Looking back, I now realize that his fresh humiliation probably caused Dad to overlook anything that might make the ride home a little more enjoyable for some of us. As a child, I never knew if such incidents would stir my father to anger or a passing moment of charity.

Whatever the case, with Frank's distaste for any discord, he would never have adapted to our home as it generally operated. It would not have been an easy home for many to adapt to.

So Frank became Bah's "hired man," even though it was for little more than three months each summer and fall. Yet after three or four years, we still knew practically nothing about this man. We only knew that when he left each autumn, we were sure to see him again the following year. We all assumed that as autumn approached, he headed south and found odd jobs to carry him through the winter months. As spring came around, he would head north again to familiar territory where he knew he could find food and a place to lay his head. Then one year the routine was irretrievably broken.

II

Christmas at Bah's

IN ADDITION TO MY DEEP ATTACHMENT TO MY grandfather, another reason I spent so much time at my grandparents' was the house itself. They had a dining room fireplace in front of which we loved to spend winter evenings popping corn. We boys would take turns holding a screen popper over the open fire while we listened to my grandfather tell stories about my ancestors. Along one wall of the dining room were cupboards that opened into the pantry where my grandmother always kept wine-drop cookies in a large stone crock. Fresh homemade pies and breads were also spread along the pantry counter, and in the cellar, which opened off the pantry, were barrels of sweet cider and bins of apples.

On the shelves between the living and dining rooms were old volumes of history books filled with illustrations from the Civil War and frontier life, a beautiful five-volume set of Cooper's *Leatherstocking Tales,* and numerous other works that set me upon the path to a love of history. Put all these ingredients together and those evenings became the best memories of my childhood.

Along with all these things, Bah and Grandma Ora had electricity, which meant being able to listen to those great radio programs of the 1930s such as *Inner Sanctum, Fibber McGee and Molly,* and *Amos 'n' Andy.* But most of all, electricity made Christmastime at my grandparents' the highlight of the year with those magical, colored Christmas tree lights.

Christmas at Bah's must have been appealing to my parents as well, because as soon as chores were completed on Christmas Eve, our family would all head for my grandparents', a mile away, to spend the entire evening and often the night.

I was nine years old the year Frank changed his routine. Both of my brothers were now gone from home. Roger was in the Marines, Duane was married, and only Louie and I were still at home with my parents.

The day before Christmas that year was typical of an upstate New York winter. It was snowing hard and I was concerned. Would we be able to go to Bah's this year? It was only a mile away, but the roads were already closed. Dad was ill-tempered and my mother was her usual silent self when he was like that. I decided to put my all into the evening chores, hoping Dad would find a way.

As we were finishing the barn work, Dad's mood suddenly improved. It was obvious that he had thought of a way to go to my grandparents'.

"Go tell your mother to get ready," he told me. I was halfway to the house before the barn door was closed. Hurrying back to the barn after telling Mom, I still didn't know how we were to get to my grandparents' unless we walked. And as excited as I was to go, walking a mile in the dark and wintry cold didn't seem particularly enticing, and my father certainly would not allow my mother to do it.

I was still somewhat puzzled when my dad took one of the lanterns and headed for the upstairs barn door. "You boys can give me a hand now," he said. Louie and I followed him, more curious than ever. Not until he started uncovering the old one-horse sleigh that hadn't been used in years did I understand how we were supposed to get to Bah's. "This is going to be even better than the old truck," I thought as I helped pull the sleigh out through the barn door.

Hitching one of our workhorses, Pat, to the sleigh, Dad was now in an uncharacteristically jovial mood. As he helped Mom into our anti-quated conveyance with a box of gifts, Louie and I needed no invitation, and soon the darkness and snow and biting cold only added to the mood of this unforgettable Christmas Eve adventure.

Pat quickly adjusted to the strange device behind him, and the roller-coaster ride over drifted banks crossing the road took us rapidly past long-familiar landmarks, now eerily disguised under darkness and falling snow. Allen's Hollow was soon passed with hardly a recognition. A perpetually dark ravine, it was said to be haunted by the spirits from a nearby graveyard whose markers had been dumped in the hollow by a farmer encroaching on the cemetery. Only the tilt of the sleigh told us we were climbing Wilcox's Hill. Turning the corner by Old Man Varn's place, we were at last on the downgrade to Bah's farm and an inviting fireside. By now the winter cold had become deep-seated, and the novelty of our old-fashioned pilgrimage was losing some of its charm.

"It's no night for travel such as this," my father observed as Pat turned into the familiar driveway by my grandfather's woodshop, "much less for one afoot." There was no disagreement as my mother and I carried the presents into the house while Louie helped Dad unharness Pat and lead him into a warm stall.

By the time I heard Dad and Louie stomping the snow from their boots in the attached woodshed, I was standing awestruck before the Christmas tree with its brilliantly colored electric lights. What a perfect night! Christmas Eve before an open fireplace, a magically illuminated tree, and the once-a-year opportunity to spend the entire night at my grandparents' home. Even with my brothers away, it was a joyous time to be together on a night that seems especially designed for families.

And tonight was just such a night. Bah's house had no central heating, so most of the house was rather chilly. But the dining room, with its brick fireplace and cozy warmth, was the family gathering place. It seemed especially snug and comforting during the harsh winter nights so common in upstate New York. As the wind moaned through the pine trees outside the dining room's north window, my grandfather piled more chunks of pungent oak on the fire. It was one of those times you want to last forever, and it only got better as Grandma Ora poured some popcorn into the wire popper. "You boys take turns now and keep it moving over the fire. You don't want to burn it!"

As Grandma Ora settled into her usual seat on the old-fashioned horsehair settee, Bah headed for the cellar to draw some cider and fill a kettle with sweet McIntosh apples from the bin in preparation for the evening storytelling.

Christmas morning wasn't really on our minds nearly as much as it must have been on my mother's. It was no longer the Depression, except on Gee Hill, where money was no less scarce than usual, so we kids weren't expecting much. I'm sure it must have bothered my mother more than Louie or me. To us it was enough to be at my grandparents' in front of an open fire, listening to Bah's stories, and eating apples and popcorn before topping off the evening with a night's sleep on a feather mattress in the little room at the top of the stairs. Tomorrow we'd all sit down to a big Christmas dinner along with my other grandmother and an uncle who'd drive out from Cortland if the roads opened. Uncle Harold, my mother's older brother, was my favorite relative next to Bah. Small, athletic, and a decorated veteran of World War I, he had just about as many stories as Bah and always made a fuss over me. An uncle like that, acting as though he enjoyed having me around, was pretty heady stuff for a nine-year-old boy.

But now it was Christmas Eve and Bah was telling stories. They were never formal. We just knew if we asked a few leading questions, he'd start, encouraged by our rapt attention. Taller than most men in our family and with a beautiful head of white hair and a mustache, Bah always had a pipe in his mouth, which he'd remove and hold in his hand as he warmed up to one of his stories.

"Tell us again about my great-uncle who led a wagon train West," I'd urge. And Bah would be off, filling in forgotten details with gory events and heroic deeds he knew would excite and intrigue us. And then perhaps he'd tell us a tale of a grandfather who had fought with General Sheridan in the Shenandoah Valley of Virginia. Bah was born shortly after the Civil War ended, so stories of that great struggle as told by relatives who had served at Shiloh and Gettysburg seemed fresh in his mind. Proof of my ancestors' brave participation was evident in the pictures he pointed out in family albums—unsmiling faces staring out from long-ago tintypes, men ramrod stiff in their Union uniforms.

In the middle of one of my grandfather's stories, a knock came on the dining room door. The sound was so faint and the night so dark and cold, it didn't seem possible someone could actually be out there in the storm. At first we thought it was a loose piece of wood on Grandma Ora's rose trellis. Certainly there could be no visitors to Gee Hill on a night like this. The roads were closed! Then we heard it again.

With a look of alarm, Grandma Ora turned to Bah. "Harry, see what that is," she urged. Laying his pipe aside, he rose from his rocker and opened the door. There, covered with snow and looking half-frozen, stood Frank, the hired man. "What in tarnation?" was all that Bah could say.

III

Christmas Mystery

IT TOOK A MINUTE FOR THE PICTURE OF FRANK standing there on the porch to register. He didn't belong here this time of year, especially on a night like this.

"Come in, come in," Bah said insistently, trying to overcome the awkwardness of the moment. Grandma Ora rose to take off Frank's thin, snow-covered knit hat and to help him off with his equally thin summer coat.

"For goodness' sake, get up here close to the fire," she coaxed. But Frank, shy in the presence of the entire family and embarrassed over the disruption his unexpected appearance had so obviously caused, fumbled for a chair away from the fire.

Looking as though he now had second thoughts about his intrusion, Frank mumbled an apology. "Didn't mean to interrupt anything" was the first and about the last full sentence he spoke that evening.

Frank was obviously uncomfortable and seemingly unwilling to tell us why he was out on a night like this, so the family thought it best to let him explain in his own due time. Although he must have been hungry, Frank was reluctant to impose any further and turned down Grandma Ora's offer of something more substantial than the apples and popcorn he reluctantly accepted. After a few futile attempts to draw him into conversation and hopefully an explanation, Bah and Grandma Ora gave up and the entire family returned to our previsitor festivities.

An occasional glance at Frank sitting off to one side showed him just as we'd come to know him, involved in his own thoughts far more than the stories and conversation that surrounded him.

As the evening wore on, our laughter seemed an intrusion on Frank and his thoughts, and he looked ill at ease with the merriment we were enjoying. My dad, who could easily converse with just about anyone except his own children, occasionally tried to draw Frank into the family circle.

"Walked far tonight?" my dad asked.

"A fair piece."

"Sure no night to be abroad," Dad continued, hoping Frank would offer further explanation.

"A mite wintry" was all he got.

Not quite willing to give up, Dad tried humor. "You're a touch early for haying, aren't you?" A fleeting but forced smile was Frank's only response, so my father abandoned further attempts to extract the reason behind Frank's unexpected Christmas Eve visit. His laborious and broken responses indicated a sadness he wasn't ready to share.

We had no way of knowing how deep his grief was or how and why such a joyful evening at my grandfather's caused only pain for Frank.

Bah had been in the middle of one of his stories when Frank had knocked at the door. As the evening's activities returned to normal, I pulled a stool up next to my grandfather's rocker and asked him to finish the story.

"Didn't I finish that?" he teased. "Where was I?"

"You were telling us about you and your dad's fishing trip down to Dryden Lake," I reminded him. It was a familiar but favorite story because it was about my great-grandfather, for whom I was named. I never knew him, but I was sure he must have been like Bah—gentle, soft-spoken, and able to fix anything.

After the Dryden Lake story about a ghost train that could still be heard from the depths of the lake into which it had plunged after derailing, Bah told us a couple of hunting stories. They all involved parents and grandparents. Life on a nineteenth-century farm in rural upstate New York could be extremely provincial, and your family was pretty much your world. It had been Bah's world, and in his quiet, unassuming way, he determined to make it our world as well. He never preached to us or even told us much about the things he believed in, but his example would have filled a book of sermons. He was a town appraiser, and when he drove his Model A around the countryside appraising farms, I was invariably with him. We didn't talk much—just being with him was enough for me. My first experience in making useful things out of pieces of wood was in his cluttered woodshop overlooking the night pasture, with him quietly showing me the proper use of tools. I can't smell freshly cut wood today without feeling his weathered hands holding mine as he guided my first use of a draw shave while I straddled the shaving horse. I remember him finishing the ax handle I had started and telling the family I had done the hardest part.

Bah was obviously my hero. But looking back, I am sure he was also my dad's. Dad was an only child, and while he was unlike my grandfather in nearly every way, he too enjoyed Bah's company, probably as much as I did. Because of my relationship with my father, I found it difficult to understand how a father and son had so much to talk about. But my dad's desire to spend so many summer evenings sitting on my grandparents' front porch in deep conversation was all right with me. It merely meant a chance for me to be with my grandfather as well.

And it was obvious Dad was enjoying his father's company on this Christmas Eve. That evening with Frank sitting off to one side was little different to me from many past Christmases spent in that room, but it was surely different for him. Where he had been spending past Christmases didn't really enter my mind, and his being here was a little odd, but under the spell of the evening, I didn't dwell on it. At one point Louie nudged me and whispered, "Frank's crying!" Glancing quickly in the hired man's direction, I noticed nothing and merely shook my head. "Old men don't cry and certainly not on a fun night like this," I thought, then tried to dismiss the thought from my mind.

A few minutes later, however, Frank quietly lifted himself from his chair and slowly walked into the darkened living room and away from the family. Conversation slowed as the adults exchanged puzzled looks, but it soon picked up again, and a few minutes later Frank emerged, his head turned from us, and seated himself in the darkened corner where the grieving of the pines outside the window could still be heard when the conversation ebbed.

Too soon bedtime came and with it an unplanned dilemma. Frank certainly couldn't be sent back into the winter night, but neither was his usual summer bedroom available. We kids would be using that. It was apparent that Frank, who for some mysterious reason had returned to his usual summer area at Christmastime, needed shelter and food. He had probably thought of my grandparents' hospitality and, not expecting the entire family to be here on Christmas Eve, had felt not too uncomfortable knocking at their door. He perhaps expected his old room at the top of the stairs would still be available, and he knew he would owe my grandparents no explanations.

"Frank, there's no extra bed, so you can stretch out here by the fire. I'll get you a couple of blankets," my grandmother offered.

"No need. I'll bed down in the stable, if that's all right?" Frank insisted, reaching for his worn coat and hat lying on a chair beside the table.

"You'll do no such thing," Grandma Ora

protested. But Frank shook his head. "I've slept in far worse places. And colder too," he insisted. Knowing the stable was warm with all that body heat from the cows, and with the soft, sweet-smelling hay at the foot of the chute to lie on, Grandma Ora reluctantly handed Frank two folded blankets. Responding with a soft "Obliged," he stepped out into the cold and headed for the barn.

"We'll call you in the morning for breakfast," my grandmother called after him, but Frank said nothing as he disappeared in the dark toward the warm stables.

As Louie and I climbed the steep stairs to the small, unheated bedroom at the top, I found it difficult not to feel a twinge of guilt for taking over what would have been Frank's room this night. And as we snuggled deep into the feather mattress, we thought of the hired man sleeping in the far less comfortable stable.

"Sure hope he's warm enough out there," I said, more to myself than Louie.

"He's used to it," Louie finally said, trying to

ease his conscience as well as mine. But I wasn't ready to dismiss the lonely old man so easily, especially on this night.

"Do you suppose he doesn't have a home?" I asked, hoping Louie could offer a response somewhat more comforting than his last one.

He didn't. "Well, he'd be there if he had one!"

Not wanting to risk another depressing reply, I dropped the subject but couldn't help thinking of Frank as we had first seen him earlier that night—eyebrows coated with ice and his hands thrust deep into the pockets of his threadbare coat. How far and how long he had struggled that winter night to reach Bah and Grandma Ora's house I could only imagine. "But he made it," I thought. "Alone in a stable on Christmas Eve isn't like a real home, but at least he's out of the cold." My conscience somewhat appeased, I drifted off to sleep.

The following morning was still dark and the cold was even more penetrating than it had been the night before. As we raced down the stairs to a warm dining room with a fire already blazing, we found our stockings hanging, as they properly should, on a real mantel. Although two-thirds filled with fruit, nuts, and popcorn balls to take up space, they were nevertheless an exciting prelude to the gifts we would open later when all the adults were up and assembled.

As my parents came out of the living room into the warm dining room, my mother remembered the hired man. "While we're waiting for your grandparents, why don't one of you children run and tell Frank to come in?"

Anticipating Frank's presence that morning, my grandmother had found a warm flannel shirt my grandfather had not yet worn and had wrapped it the night before. It was under the tree with Frank's name on it.

Excited by the prospect of sharing Christmas morning with our melancholy but gentle visitor, Louie and I rushed for the woodshed where our outdoor clothes were hanging. The frigid morning air took our breath away as we opened the outside door and sprinted for the barn. Across the barn floor and down the stable stairs we raced, expecting to catch the old man still asleep on the pile of hay at the foot of the stairs. To our surprise, only the two blankets were there, still carefully folded as they had been when Grandma Ora had handed them to Frank the night before.

Even as the words "Where is he?" escaped my mouth, I knew it was a foolish question. The old man was gone. For some reason, he hadn't even stayed the night. But why? Louie and I just looked at one another. With Frank's disappearance, a little of the joy of that particular Christmas seemed to vanish with him. In my youthful mind, I somehow sensed I wouldn't be seeing him again, not even when haying season rolled around. His wordless departure was a good-bye.

Back to the house we trudged with the two blankets and news of Frank's unexplained departure. No one had much to say except Grandma Ora.

"Well, doesn't that beat all! And on a night like last night! Why would he leave? Where would he go?" she asked no one in particular.

Ignoring the question, my mother turned to Louie and me. "Are you sure he wasn't someplace else there in the barn?"

"Mom, the hay hadn't even been slept on," I

answered. I turned to look at my grandfather for an explanation.

Bah didn't say a word, but I imagine he was thinking what I was thinking. Frank wasn't coming back and we'd miss his gentle strength and quiet ways next summer. He had walked into our lives one hot summer day and he had walked out of them one cold Christmas Eve night.

When the haying season began the following summer, no one was surprised when Frank didn't show up. Several opinions were expressed, but they were just guesses of course.

Louie and I dramatically imagined Frank freezing to death the night he left and never being found. Grandma Ora was sure he'd finally found a full-time job with a permanent room of his own. Dad and Bah figured he had merely changed his summer routine, wandering a new part of the country. Whatever the case, he remained one of those little intriguing mysteries that offered some interesting speculations during front-porch summer evenings after an exhausting day loading and unloading hay. Frank would have been a big help, especially with both my older brothers now away at war.

But I don't think we really wanted to know what had happened to him. Facts have a way of ruining some interesting hypotheses. And then as the years went by, thoughts of Frank faded.

IV

Curmudgeon

WE EVENTUALLY GOT ELECTRICITY IN THE
homeplace and no longer went to Bah and
Grandma Ora's for Christmas. My brothers both
returned safely from World War II, but married
and had their own homes. And when Louie was
seventeen, he left to work in a carnival with his
real mother. Although neither my father nor the
family was aware of it at the time, Dad was in
what we later found out was the early stages of
lung cancer, which would eventually take his life.
We all knew something was wrong, but our family

doctor was too inexperienced to detect the cancer as it developed. My mother continually urged my dad to try another doctor, but he stubbornly refused and continued paying out hard-earned dollars for useless medication as the slow-moving disease took more and more of his strength.

Because of my dad's ill health and lack of farm help, we cut back considerably on our farmwork. We rented much of our land to a neighbor, and Dad got a less strenuous job driving a school bus. So from about fourteen on, I was alone with my parents.

I still visited Bah and Grandmas Ora's from time to time, but it wasn't the same. Bah hadn't changed; I still loved him deeply. But I was a teenager now, reluctant to demonstrate the idolization I'd been so open with as a young child. Besides, I was spending more and more time in school sports and with my friends.

Dad, who had always been quick-tempered and difficult to communicate with, became even more distant from me as I went through my early "know-it-all" teen years. We disagreed about anything and everything, and when I entered my later teens, we couldn't communicate at all—even to argue. I was still unaware that my dad's illness would eventually prove fatal, but he must have sensed that he would never regain his health. Because of his illness, and consequently an awareness of his mortality, Dad had become far less volatile, but our relationship just seemed too far gone to ever mend.

As a teenager, at times I felt he existed to prevent any happiness I might find. That was the case with the happiness my fifteen-year-old self was sure I could find with Cynthia Noughton, who lived in the valley east of Gee Hill. By road it was at least seven or eight miles from our farm to hers, but it was less than a mile straight over the big hill behind our place. The distance may have been the reason I didn't meet her until I was a young teenager—that and the fact that our families had been feuding with each other for years. It was not a Hatfield-McCoy battle that all the neighbors were aware of, but rather one that started when my brother Duane got into a fight with Patric, one of the Noughton boys, when they were both quite young. Every time it looked as if Duane would win the fight, Mr. Noughton would interfere by pulling him off Patric and putting Patric back on top of my brother. Duane never forgot the incident nor forgave Mr. Noughton, and when Duane was about seventeen, he walked over the hill, called Mr. Noughton out of his house, and beat him for his interference years earlier.

And that, apparently, was the basis for the feud, in which my dad uncharacteristically supported Duane. Since I was younger and had had nothing to do with the incident, I never felt I needed to be part of the private war. I felt even less inclined when I first met Cynthia, Patric's younger sister who was about my age.

The chance meeting took place when I was fifteen and we got a call from Mr. Noughton telling us our cows had escaped and wandered over the hill to his farm. He urged my father in no uncertain terms to remove our livestock or he'd drive them even farther away. We always responded immediately when our cows got loose, but in this case the cows were farther away, the call was less friendly, and of all places, it was the Noughton farm where they'd ended up. So this time not only did we respond immediately, but we practically ran the mile over the hill to recover our stock. I had never been to the Noughton farm before, so I anticipated an angry farmer with perhaps a couple of angry sons. Instead of two angry sons, however, there were two quite attractive daughters, and one of them appeared to be about my age. They helped us get the animals started for home, which gave me a chance to find out Cynthia's name. She was also fifteen, and when I hesitantly suggested, "Maybe I'll see you again," she quietly responded, "Why not?" With a beautiful Irish smile under her red hair, she followed her younger sister back to their farm.

A couple of days later, as I struck out on one of my evening groundhog hunts, which I went on more to avoid spending the evening with my dad than to actually do any hunting, I crossed over the big hill. My unusual bravado faded as I approached the Noughton farm. Fortunately, Cynthia was in the yard, and her pleasant smile gave me the confidence to easily find words to begin my first romance, which, in my youthful mind, was also going to be my only. We talked easily about many things, even the feud, which seemed silly to both of us. It was almost dark when I reluctantly started for home and was fully dark when I stepped onto the back porch. Dad and Mom were still at the supper table as I entered.

"Rather late to be hunting, isn't it?" Dad asked, not really expecting an answer and not getting one. As I sat down to eat a late supper, he got up and went into the dining room.

Thus began my fifteenth summer. I'd spend exhausting days working on a family farm that was rapidly going downhill, then spend two or three evenings a week supposedly clearing Gee Hill of woodchucks. Instead of hunting, however, I'd be out for long walks with Cynthia or sitting in the tree swing behind her house. Her father soon realized that his daughter was too young for the relationship she seemed to be developing and certainly too young to be developing it with a member of our family.

Late one evening in August, as we were sitting by a small brook that meandered along the dusty road below the Noughton home, Cynthia broke the news. I remember we were sitting with our feet in the shallow brook, and she stared into the water for several minutes before speaking.

"My dad says we can't see each other anymore." Without waiting for my obvious reply of "Why not?" she continued, "He says we're too serious and too young." As I stuttered out an objection and a confused and angry "What?" she said, "He went to see your father this afternoon."

Cynthia's good-night kiss was not as pleasurable as it usually was. My mind was churning as the reality of our helplessness sank in. I had no idea of what to expect when I got home, but the memory of my father waiting there for me is as deeply embedded as the memory of Cynthia standing near the creek where I'd left her. As I entered our cheerless home, I was met with a stony silence and then, "No more trips to the Noughtons'—especially the Noughtons'—for as long as you live here. That's final."

And it was.

By the time I was nineteen, I had started school at the College of Agriculture at Cornell University but dropped out after my first year. I decided I didn't want to be a farmer and work hard for little or nothing as Dad and Bah had. I suppose Dad was disappointed. He was uncharacteristically proud when I started college, but I didn't realize the extent of his fatherly pride until after I quit.

I had stopped one afternoon for gas at Tripp's service station in Dryden, where my dad drove a school bus, when I ran into Johnny, who worked with my father.

"I hear you quit college." He smiled when he said it. "How come?"

"Just wasn't for me, I guess," I replied, not wanting to be taken for a quitter.

"Your dad must be quite disappointed."

I looked at Johnny in surprise. "I don't know. He hasn't mentioned it to me. Has he said something?"

"No, but he sure was proud when you started college," he said matter-of-factly.

"Was he? I never noticed."

"Well, he showed us all your letter of admission and said you were the first in your family to ever go to college. That was all he talked about for two or three days."

As I started my car and pulled away from the pumps that day, I thought about what Johnny had said. Maybe that explained the argument I'd had with my dad a few days after I told Mom I wasn't going back to the Ag College. The argument was over some obscure politician my dad liked and I didn't. At the time I didn't understand his vehement anger over such a minor issue. Now it made sense. Dad had said nothing when I quit college—he probably didn't want to say anything because he had quit high school—but he was disappointed and displeased by my decision and it had simply come to the surface during our political disagreement.

That argument had been so bitter I considered leaving home. My mother, as usual, had patched things up and I stayed on. But I resolved to get a job away from the farm.

"But it's not just the farming," I thought. "I don't want to be like him. When I'm proud of someone, I'll tell him." But looking back, I saw I was like him. He had worked hard all his life on a hardscrabble clay-hill farm for his family, and I had never told him I understood and appreciated and was proud of his integrity and selfless toil, in spite of his shortcomings. I took comfort in the thought that few teenagers would ever tell a parent that sort of thing.

Determined, however, to live a life different from his, I was home from college only a couple of weeks when I found a job driving a petroleum delivery truck for a farm cooperative. It was dirty and boring work, but it gave me enough money to be semi-independent—meaning I slept at home but spent any spare time away from home on dates, with friends, or just "hanging out." Whenever I thought of it, I gave my mother a few dollars a week for room and board. When I forgot, she never reminded me. She was always more concerned about the relationship between my dad and me. He and I still had little if anything in common and avoided each other—usually.

The exception might be on my arrival home on Sunday or Monday mornings just as he was getting up. He couldn't resist a scowl and a brief comment, which I would pointedly ignore.

"I wish you'd understand your father," Mom would say. "He does love you."

"Well, he's never told me and he has a funny way of showing it," I'd reply, not terribly concerned, but subconsciously wishing it were different. I just didn't remember us ever having any good conversations. I only remembered him chastising and criticizing, which perhaps I deserved to a large extent. Even the "good times" were always edged with the knowledge that they wouldn't last long.

My job kept me busy five and a half days a week, delivering tractor fuel to farmers and heating oil to homeowners. So between my work and my social life, I didn't have much time to spend at home or even to think about how my folks were feeling about the nearly empty house that had before been filled with sons and foster children. But with Christmas approaching that year, I should have. In earlier years I had certainly shared some of the joys of Christmas, especially with my mother, as we decorated the dining room with garlands and red and green paper bells. I know she enjoyed it when I pretended to supervise the baking of Christmas cookies and the making of my favorite candies. Dad's Christmas contribution began and ended with his bringing home the tree and making a wooden stand for it. But it didn't matter. In earlier years it was exciting just to have a vacation from school and to count down the days to Christmas.

But Christmastime is not necessarily a joyfully anticipated day when one is nineteen years old— at least it wasn't for me. I now felt too old to get excited about Christmas mornings anymore, and I was sobered by the realization of how meager our Depression Christmases had been with so little to open and even less to give. And I didn't yet have my own family, so there were no little ones for whom Christmas seemed intended.

The day before Christmas this particular year, as I left for work, my mother, trying to be casual, asked, "Will you be home early tonight?" She must have been thinking of the way our Christmases used to be.

"I've got my regular full route, so it'll probably

be around the same time," I replied, trying desperately to think of some unmade plan for the evening that would prevent me from having to spend it alone with my folks in such a cheerless home.

"I'm not sure though about my plans for tonight," I added, immediately regretting my words as my mother turned to hide her look of disappointment.

Not knowing what more I could now say to make amends for those words, and even wanting to believe I had misinterpreted her expression, I quickly closed the door behind me.

It was not a good day. At every stop on my route there was anticipation of family get-togethers and a holiday mood that I resented more and more as the day progressed.

Dusk was just coming on as I made my last delivery to a home on the edge of the little town of East Homer. After pumping the fuel oil, I tabulated the bill and went to the kitchen door to collect.

"Step inside while I get you a check," the lady of the house told me as she disappeared into another room to find her checkbook. Standing in the warm kitchen with its odors of holiday baking brought back an unwelcome flood of memories.

As I glanced around the colorfully decorated house, I noticed through the living room door a large evergreen with presents piled beneath. Someplace out of sight I heard the excited laughter and chatter of several children. An elderly man came through the door. "My daughter asked me to give you this," he said as he handed me the check. "Would you like some refreshments?"

"I don't think so. Thanks anyway," I mumbled, and retreated quickly from his genial "Merry Christmas!"

"What a worn-out cliché," I thought to myself as I climbed into the cab of the truck and pulled out of the driveway.

Those last two or three miles back to the plant, I felt I was at the low point in my life. Here it was my first Christmas Eve with the anticipation of money in my pocket and my own car, and I had no place I wanted to go and nothing I wanted to do on what should be and used to be the most anticipated night of the year for me.

My friends were spending Christmas with their

families, my usual haunts were closed for the holiday, and my own home, sadly, wasn't especially inviting. Brothers or sisters there might have made some difference, but the thought of spending the evening at home with a father I couldn't talk to was more depressing than the thought of spending it alone.

V

Lost and Found

MOST OF THE DRIVERS WERE ALREADY IN when I pulled my truck into the petroleum plant at Polkville. Backing into the garage, I grabbed my tally sheet and money bag and headed for the office to cash in and pick up my weekly paycheck.

The office was bustling with the other drivers hurrying to complete their paperwork and head home to their families for Christmas Eve. I wasn't in any hurry.

As I was waiting my turn at one of the adding

machines, our boss, Bucky, was taking a call on the office phone. "Are you sure you don't have enough to last two more days?" he was asking. After a pause he said, "But this is Christmas Eve."

There was another pause, and then turning to those of us still in the office, he hollered, "Anyone want to make a fuel oil delivery in Marathon?"

"What a stupid question," we all thought. It was like asking, "Who wants to miss Christmas Eve with their families?"

Knowing I was the only single guy in the company, everyone turned to me. I wasn't anxious to get home, but neither was I too excited about getting my truck back out, filling it with fuel oil, and driving a twenty-five-mile round-trip to help out some guy who didn't check his fuel oil gauge until Christmas Eve.

"I'll take it," I finally mumbled, knowing Bucky would have to take it if there were no volunteers. He had a family also. "What the heck," I thought as I headed for the garage. "This will just use up some of the long evening I wasn't looking forward to anyway."

Feeling somewhat guilty for sending one of his drivers back out on this particular night, Bucky climbed to the fuel tank platform to guide the fuel spout into my truck tank as I drove up. After he finished he slapped my cab top and yelled, "Thanks!"

I pulled out of the yard and headed south on Route 11 toward Marathon. This wasn't my regular route, but with the street address Bucky handed me, I wasn't too concerned about finding the right house.

Traffic was light. "Guess everyone's home with their families," I mused, not sure if the thought was pleasant or not. But the roads were clear—not like some Christmas Eves I remembered as my mind drifted back to those family get-togethers at Bah and Grandma Ora's.

As I hit the town limits of Marathon, my formerly dark mood was replaced by a mixed bag of nostalgia over past Christmases, self-satisfying pleasure over helping out my friends, and frustration with forgetful homeowners.

"I hope Bucky got these directions right," I thought aloud as I turned right at the first traffic signal and drove across the river looking for the street name he had jotted down. And there it was—first one on the left.

Taking the turn, I found the house as described and pulled into the driveway. "His tank better be close to empty," I grumbled to myself as I set the brake, climbed down from the cab, and headed across the snow-covered lawn.

"It's a 275-gallon tank," the gentleman who answered my knock told me. "The filler pipe is close to your truck by the side of the house. You might as well fill it."

"You bet I'll fill it and make it worth my while," I muttered, heading for the back of the truck and the hose reel. "After coming all the way down here on Christmas Eve!"

Stamping my feet on the snow-covered lawn to keep them warm, I waited in the biting cold for the gurgling sound in the filler pipe, telling me the tank was full. It came sooner than I expected. I closed the cap on the pipe and dragged the end of the hose back to the truck to reel it in, glancing at the gauge as I did.

"Wouldn't you know it! Slightly over two hundred gallons. He had plenty of oil for several more days. I should charge him extra."

But as I made out the bill, I didn't. "In fact I won't even mention it to him—in the spirit of Christmas," I reflected sarcastically. "He'll notice when he sees the amount of the bill and that should be enough to embarrass him."

If he noticed, he said nothing, and I thought nothing more about it myself after what transpired over the next several minutes.

Another knock on the door to give him the bill and pick up the money was quickly answered. But this time it wasn't the man of the house. It was, I assumed, his daughter, a girl about my age. I immediately recognized her as Diane, a young woman I had met on a nearby farm in July when I was filling in on that route for a sick driver. I had stopped to ask directions of some men working in a field just as she had stopped to deliver something to one of the workers. We had struck up a conversation as we walked back to our vehicles. She was rather attractive and had given me her name and requested phone number, which I had never followed up on. In fact, her last name hadn't even rung any bells with me when Bucky gave me the name and address for the delivery.

But what made this Christmas Eve so memorable was not meeting her again; it was what occurred as I stood just inside the door talking to her. Between the entry and the living room were double French doors, and my eyes were drawn to the scene beyond them. In the corner was a large, brilliantly lit Christmas tree, and standing near it were two men. Some women and children were in the room also, but the two men caught my attention. Or perhaps I should say it was one of those two men.

He was close to my grandfather's age. Bah was now about seventy-four. In fact, the old gentleman reminded me at first of my grandfather—roughly the same height and with white hair. But it was something else. He looked so familiar and yet I knew he wasn't anyone I had met recently. It was like a flashback to someone I must have known years before. And then suddenly I remembered.

"But it can't be," I told myself. I couldn't believe it.

"The old gentleman by the tree . . . who is

he?" I asked, interrupting something Diane was saying.

Turning to follow my gaze, she answered in a puzzled voice, "My grandfather. Why?"

"He looks like someone I knew a long time ago."

Diane smiled. "A long time ago you were pretty young."

"I know," I replied, still looking at the older man. "But that's when I think it was."

I turned back to Diane. She wasn't smiling anymore. Instead she asked in a rather serious tone, "Where do you think you met him?"

We were interrupted by her father, who turned toward us. "Diane. Any problem?"

In answer, she turned, walked into the room, and handed him my bill. Coming back, she said, "He'll have a check for you in a minute. Now, where did you say you'd seen my grandfather?"

She was strangely insistent. But now I knew for sure. When Diane had gone into the living room, the older man had turned to face us and I knew it was Frank, my granddad's sometime hired man, the summer hobo.

I didn't know how to answer. "It doesn't make sense," I thought.

Why would her grandfather have been roaming the country like a hobo? And that Christmas Eve at my grandparents' home . . . why would he . . . My thoughts were interrupted by an obviously bewildered but still determined Diane.

"Well? Where was he?"

Trying to sort out my tangled thoughts, all I could think of was "He used to work for my granddad, I believe."

The answer didn't satisfy Diane. She wanted more details, which I thought strange. Didn't the family know anything about Frank's bohemian life?

What I remembered about Frank was far more positive than negative, so I hesitantly told her what I recalled. It wasn't difficult making Frank out to be a virtuous, kind, and hardworking nomad, which is what I recalled most about him.

We were interrupted again when Diane's brother came to the entry and handed me a check with a knowing grin. "Go on now," she told him, scowling. As he headed back to the living room, she again turned to me. "Where and when did you last see him?"

Her question prompted the memory of Christmas Eve exactly ten years ago, to the very night.

Since it was obvious Diane never knew, I felt compelled to tell her about the night Frank came in from a wintry storm, spent the evening with our family, and then mysteriously disappeared.

As I related that memorable night so many years ago, tears came to Diane's eyes. Normally one or both of us should have been embarrassed, but we weren't. We were interrupted again when Diane's father turned and called, "Diane!"

Reaching for the handle of the doors between us and the living room, she merely replied, "I'll be in shortly." As she pulled the doors closed, her dad smiled and turned back to Frank. Motioning me to sit down next to her on a narrow bench in the entry, Diane tearfully told me her story, and now after ten years, the mystery of the hired man's Christmas began to clear up.

Apparently, her father and grandfather had had a falling-out over some long-ago forgotten issue when Diane and her brothers were quite young. At least Diane had never been told the cause, but she had been told that her father and grandfather had always found communication difficult. Her grandmother had passed away shortly before the "falling-out," and Frank had come to live with his son and family. Perhaps the grief of Frank's losing both his beloved wife and his independence at the same time aggravated the relationship between father and son. Anyhow, the tension escalated, she had been told, and one day after a particularly bitter argument her grandfather packed a few belongings in a small bag and walked out. Frank's family didn't know, when he walked out, that he was planning to walk out of their lives for good.

Thinking he had perhaps simply gone to visit other relatives or a friend while the dispute cooled, the family made no effort to check on those possibilities for several days. When they finally checked with friends and family, they discovered that not a soul had seen or heard from him. Diane said her father, still grieving over the loss of his mother and then tormented by the guilt of having "driven" his father out, spent the next several months searching, writing letters, and advertising for news of his father's whereabouts—all to no avail.

Reluctantly, the family came to accept the double loss and life went on for the next few years. It went on, but it wasn't quite the same. Diane's mother used to describe the good times the family had had when both of Diane's grandparents were alive, and the family gatherings on holidays, especially Christmas. They continued to celebrate with the usual festivities as far as Diane knew, but older relatives said it just wasn't the same with Frank gone.

"Didn't you remember him?" I asked.

"Yeah. Some things." Diane turned to look at her grandfather through the French doors. "I especially remembered him at Christmas when the whole family got together as we are tonight. And that seemed to be when we missed him the most. But Dad didn't want to talk about him. I guess he felt so guilty about causing him to leave."

Frank had been the patriarch, the link to the family's past. He served as the keeper of the flame, filled with ancestor stories and history that give meaning to the entire concept of *family*. When he disappeared, it was as though a memory had fragmented, and the present became less meaningful because an important part of the family's story couldn't be told.

When Diane's grandmother had died, there was a finalization of her mortal life and a meaningful ending, but Frank's disappearance had no ending. He was not there with the family, but neither was he gone. The whole family, especially Diane's father, could not come to terms with the loss. But mainly, they just missed his gentle presence and fatherly strength.

As Diane soberly finished telling me what her grandfather's absence had meant, she hesitated. We had been talking there in front of the door for some time and my truck was still running. But her story wasn't finished.

"And then?" I asked.

Her voice broke as she started to relate what happened that Christmas night when she was nine or ten years old. She remembered the night vividly, but not the year.

She hesitated as she wiped tears from her eyes,

and for the first time she seemed embarrassed about showing her emotions. Not wanting to look at me, she stared through the closed doors in the direction of her grandfather. I wanted to put my arms around her as I thought of all those good years I had spent with my own grandfather. I could only reach out, however, and gently touch her clasped hands. Turning back and looking down, she continued.

"It was about three or four o'clock in the morning when our front doorbell woke up the whole family. It had been a bitterly cold and snowy night, and Dad had been teasing us about Santa not coming because of the weather. We kids all thought the noise had something to do with Christmas, and we all came out of our bedrooms to investigate while Dad answered the door.

"It was Grampa Frank!" Diane's voice broke as she must have pictured the sight of her grandfather, an exhausted and shivering old man, barely able to stand after that long walk in the stormy darkness from our farm twelve miles away. It was one of the few times she remembers her father crying as he threw his arms around his father there in that very entry where Diane and I were now talking.

Diane stopped, a wistful look in her eyes as she described her grandfather's Christmas home-coming.

"I never saw my dad so happy. I remember not even caring what I got for Christmas that morn-ing. My grandfather was home and that's all that mattered to the whole family."

Frank was home, but life did not return to nor-mal. Normal, before Frank's disappearance, had included bickering and criticisms and petty quar-rels. Diane related how her grandfather's long absence and final return had brought the family closer than ever. It had put life's important things, such as love and kindness and consideration, into a more eternal perspective.

"Did your grandfather ever tell anyone about where he'd been all those years?" I asked.

"I don't know. If my father ever found out, he never told me," Diane whispered as she shook her head. But now she knew for the first time where her grandfather had spent a part of those lonely years. And she also knew as I did what must have prompted him to finally return home to his own family.

It might already have been on his mind. Perhaps he just couldn't take another Christmas away from his family but didn't know how to return. Perhaps that was why he had returned to my grandfather's home—to finally unburden himself to someone he knew and respected. Whether he would have said anything to my grandfather that evening if the rest of the family had not been there, we'll never know. But that Christmas Eve spent silently observing our family around the fire and the warmth of the family relationship had undoubtedly convinced Frank to forget the past and sent him walking twelve miles through a cold, wintry night to be with his family again. And then suddenly the irony struck me. The same family that had compelled Frank to go home ten years earlier was the same family I was running from tonight.

"Well, my truck is still running and you've

got to get back to your family." I slowly rose, not wanting to leave this special home or Diane, but there seemed little more to say.

"Will I see you again?" she asked. I wasn't sure whether she really wanted to or she didn't know what else to say. Whatever the case, it didn't seem appropriate to pursue the topic this night, so I merely nodded and turned to the door.

VI

Journey Back

As I stepped out into the night, I noticed it didn't seem quite as cold as when I had first knocked on the door. Perhaps it was just my imagination or the comforting thought of an easy drive back to the plant in a warm truck.

That was the last I ever saw of Diane or her grandfather. I have driven through Marathon many times since that Christmas Eve when I was nineteen, and I seldom do so without thinking of Bah's hired man and the Christmas Eve he spent with our family. And the picture of the hired man's cold, lonely walk home through that dark winter night has ever since become my yardstick for understanding the phrase *power of love.*

I remember the return trip to the petroleum plant that night and the emotions that washed over me. I thought of the new respect I had for Diane's father, who had never learned to read an oil tank gauge but had learned not too late the real meaning of family love; of Diane, with whom I now shared some special knowledge; and of Frank. No, he wasn't the hired man I remembered sitting on the bed in the little room at the top of the stairs on that rainy summer day, just staring out the window, unwilling to acknowledge my presence. He had become a father and a grandfather, longing for his family as he looked off in the direction of his son's home a mere twelve miles to the south. He was no longer simply ignoring a young boy at his bedroom door; he just couldn't trust himself to say anything to a youngster who probably brought back memories of his own son when their relationship was still full of hope for the future.

No, Frank was no longer merely a mysterious

hobo who had been Bah's part-time hired man. He had become a unique individual—not so unlike my own father and grandfather—who behind his seemingly unsociable exterior had a deep longing for the company of those he loved. My recollection of Frank would be forever consigned to a special part of my memory, like a religious experience that loses its sacredness if exposed to the casual listener.

But mainly that night, as I drove back along the nearly deserted highway to the plant, my thoughts went to my own father and the "falling-out" we had experienced as I grew older. For the first time that day I thought of him and my mother alone on Christmas Eve. In the best of times ours was a primitive and rather cheerless home, and tonight it would be even more so with my dad, still in his fifties, dying from a disease not yet diagnosed, and my mother's world, as limited as it had always been, becoming even smaller as her last son sought to escape. Still, it was the only home I had known. I was born in the small, unheated bedroom my mother still shared with my dad. My mother, I had discovered years after my birth, had desperately wanted a daughter and had even selected a name for her. When the doctor told her she could have no more children after me, she realized she would never have that daughter to share her joys, her loneliness, and her hard labor in that simple hillside farmhouse. My mother certainly deserved better from me than my absence on Christmas Eve. "And Dad?" I groped for some memories of experiences we had shared that might reveal the kind of love that took the hired man home that night. And for the first time in years, some early, fragmented memories of my father came to the surface.

One of the earliest was of me sitting in his lap in a large wicker rocking chair, with a blanket around both of us, close to a glowing, potbellied woodstove, and listening to the winter wind blowing against our hillside home. Then, rising to the surface came the memory of my dad holding his arms under me while trying to teach me to swim in the stock pond, and how he smiled as I made my first solo strokes the few feet back to the bank. And then unaccustomed tears came to my eyes as I recalled an incident on a nearby farm one summer day. I had accompanied my dad, who, along with several neighbors, had joined to help a temporarily disabled farmer do his haying.

My dad was mowing in a nearby field while several of the other men were getting ready to haul some hay. One of the men had noticed a nest of yellow jackets on the edge of the field, and they were all standing back looking at them when I, no older than four or five, approached to see what they were looking at. Thinking it might be fun, one of the men pushed me toward the nest. Immediately, the bees attacked. Terrified and screaming from the stings, I ran toward my father in the field. Seeing me running and crying, he stopped the horses, jumped from the mower, and ran to meet me. Picking me up, he quickly determined what had happened, his face turning red with anger. Saving that anger for a later confrontation I only heard about, he carried me to a nearby stream where he mixed some mud and tenderly applied it to the swellings on my face and arms. I don't know whether it was the mud or his soothing voice as he held me that made the pain go away, but as I thought back to the event, I could feel his arms around me there in the cab of the truck on that Christmas Eve.

Somehow the Christmas lights in the windows of the homes I passed on my trip back to the plant didn't look quite the same now. I no longer resented this night that was so special to so many.

"I wonder what those lights must have looked like to Frank as he struggled past them on that wintry night ten years ago. Did he even notice them? What love that journey home to his son expressed," I thought.

But immediately my thoughts slipped from Frank back to my own father again. Those memories of my father a few minutes earlier had been when I was very young.

"What happened as I got older?" I wondered. "Did he love me less or just have trouble expressing it?"

As I watched the plowed snowbanks along Route 11 slipping past my truck, my mind wandered back to a cold, snowy January morning when I was about twelve years old.

Roger, who had joined the Marines in 1942 at the age of seventeen, was somewhere in the Pacific fighting the Japanese. My brother Duane had joined the paratroops and had returned home on furlough briefly before leaving for the war in Europe.

Dad had driven Mom and me to the Greyhound bus station in Cortland that morning to see Duane off. In my excitement at being seen with my big brother in his paratrooper uniform, I undoubtedly failed to consider the bitterness of the occasion for my parents. Of their three sons, two would now be in combat thousands of miles away. I was the only child still safe at home.

As we said our good-byes that morning, my mother's eyes were red from weeping. Dad appeared to be his usual stoic self as the bus pulled away. Nothing was said as we walked back to our old Chevy and I climbed into the backseat. Driving up Clinton Avenue, we turned left on Main instead of continuing across and out Groton Avenue toward home as I expected.

As we pulled into a parking space in front of Mullen's Stationery store, I became more curious.

Dad and Mom had said nothing about doing any shopping, and somehow it didn't seem like an appropriate thing to be doing on that day.

As Dad got out of the car, he pulled the seat forward.

"Come on, George," he said, waving his hand for me to follow him.

"Where are we going?" I asked, noting my mother was making no move to get out of the car. I was even more perplexed when she gave my father a resigned look and murmured, "You know we can't afford it."

Without answering, Dad crossed the sidewalk with me in tow. I didn't remember ever being inside Mullen's, but I had more than once stood in front of the store looking in the plate-glass window at the display of expensive-looking books. But new books were a luxury our family couldn't afford. Several times on rainy Saturday afternoons, my dad had taken me to a secondhand shop on Groton Avenue and we'd picked out a ten-cent hardback by Zane Grey or James Oliver Curwood or Jack London or some such author.

So I still couldn't imagine what Dad had in mind as the salesman approached.

"What may I do for you?" he asked, undoubtedly not expecting to do much for the humbly dressed farmer before him.

The salesman and I were both a little surprised when Dad answered, "I'd like to see that Audubon book in the window."

Trying unsuccessfully to disguise his feelings about what he obviously considered an exercise in futility, the clerk reached into the display and handed Dad a large folio volume of *Birds of America*. "It's rather expensive," the clerk warned. "About six dollars." Wincing slightly, Dad said, "We'll take it."

I was no less astonished than the salesman, especially with Dad's use of the word *we'll*, indicating that in some way I might be included in the book's ownership. My hopes were verified when, after paying for the book, Dad handed it to me and said only, "Let's go home."

What Dad and Mom had to sacrifice for that six dollars I'll never know. It's paid off handsomely, however, when even now I try to balance some of my harsh childhood experiences with my father by opening that same book and looking at the flyleaf. Dad couldn't even bring himself to inscribe it. He left it to Mom to write, "George from Dad, Jan. 18, 1944."

I guess it just wasn't part of Dad's nature to express tender emotions or demonstrate any regret for past harshness. As my nostalgic mood prompted me to think more about him, however, I could recall a few of his awkward attempts to let me know he was uneasy about some things in the past. For the first time I felt able to put meaning to an uncomfortable hospital scene that had occurred when I was sixteen years old. Dad, his body weakened by the slow cancerous growth, had come down with pneumonia and, for the first time in his life, he ended up in a hospital.

It was a warm spring day, and having just acquired my junior driver's license, I offered to take Mom to see Dad in the Cortland Hospital. As we entered the ward, I hung back several feet, not only because I seldom had much to communicate to my father, but also because seeing him under that oxygen tent caused some unpleasant mixed emotions. The father who had always seemed so harsh now appeared so helpless. Maybe I hadn't done my part to demonstrate any compassion or charity; I could be stubborn also.

He was awake as we approached his bed, and his eyes seemed to reflect a sadness I was not used to. Perhaps he thought he was dying, but that thought didn't cross my mind at the time. As despotic as he may have seemed to me, my mother needed him and I was sure he would soon be home.

"George brought me to see you," Mom said, as usual trying to improve the relationship between her husband and youngest son. A faint smile crossed his face as he murmured, "I'm glad." He and Mom did all the conversing as I stood near the foot of the bed. He was weak, however, and Mom did most of the talking. She filled him in on news from Gee Hill and the farm and how my older brothers were spending most of their spare time from their own jobs helping out.

As we prepared to leave, Dad moved his hand across the bed toward me. "I've been thinking," he said. "That Noughton girl . . . if you want to use the car . . ." I couldn't help smiling as I remembered his severity only the year before when he had forbidden me to see her. "It's all right," I interrupted. "There's someone else—at school—a cheerleader." I wanted to say more about her, but not to Dad. He looked at me, expecting more, and seemed disappointed when I added nothing. Only now did I begin to regret not having continued that opening and also not having taken his hand when he moved it toward me. "Might that have made some kind of difference?" I wondered as I slowed the truck and turned into the plant driveway.

"No, this is certainly not the night to be away from home," I concluded as I again backed my truck into its stall at Polkville. Heading for my car, after closing and locking the overhead door, I glanced at my watch under the yard lights. It still wasn't too late to spend Christmas Eve at home.

Crossing Main Street in Cortland and heading out Tompkins Street toward home, I reflected on how little Cortland had changed since I was much younger. I used to enjoy Christmas shopping with my mother even though we had little to spend. I guess she enjoyed as much as I did the sights and sound of Christmas in what to us was a big city. Wandering through the stores, trying to match my extremely limited resources with appropriate small gifts for my folks and grandparents, was a joyful challenge. I don't remember even visiting the toy sections of stores at Christmastime. Perhaps my mother purposely steered me clear of such temptations, knowing her limited ability to meet my desires, but also knowing how much more important it was to teach me the joy of giving to others.

Passing out of the city limits on Route 13 headed south, I was reliving those Christmas shopping trips with my mother when a terrible thought suddenly hit me.

Although it wouldn't be much, I knew my parents had spent some hard-earned dollars to have something under the tree for me on Christmas morning. What had happened to the joy of giving that my mother had tried to instill in me? I had been so filled with negative and depressing thoughts about Christmas, I hadn't thought about my parents' Christmas. I didn't have a single gift to give them.

VII

Homecoming

MAKING A U-TURN ON THE ALMOST DESERTED highway, I headed back to town. As I turned up Main Street, my heart sank. The stores were closed of course. It was after nine o'clock on Christmas Eve, and the merchants had shut down early to spend that important evening with their families. I drove the entire length of Main and then up Groton Avenue, looking desperately for a store, any store, that was still open where I could find something for my folks. But even if I did find one, would they take an uncashed paycheck?

Circling around West Main, I headed back toward the main shopping area. Even an all-night drugstore would do, but there was nothing. I was almost back to Tompkins Street again, panic-stricken at the thought of receiving something from my folks and giving nothing in return. Suddenly, there was the Tobacco Shop looking as if it might be open.

Making another U-turn on the deserted street, I parked in front of the store. Sure enough, someone was behind the counter. I had no idea what they might have that would be appropriate for my mother, but I knew they had knives and fishing gear and hunting magazines for my dad.

"Evening" was the jovial greeting as I pushed open the door. No other customers were in the store.

"Getting ready to close?" I asked, knowing it wouldn't take long to browse through his small inventory.

"Take your time," he responded without really answering my question.

"Must be he has no family to spend Christmas Eve with," I thought to myself. "Or he needs everything he can make, to be open this late on Christmas Eve."

"One more question—will you take a company check? I haven't had time to cash it."

Glancing at the check I handed him, he nodded. "Sure. What can I help you with?"

A little too embarrassed to explain my foolish tardiness in shopping for my parents at nine o'clock on Christmas Eve, I merely replied, "Let me look around."

"This fellow must have stocked this shop just for me," I thought as I glanced around. Aside from the traditional gifts for men, he had clocks and toasters and even inexpensive jewelry. He had apparently added a lot of special merchandise to his normal inventory just for the Christmas season.

As I starting laying items on the counter, I told the old fellow to stop me when the paycheck ran out. This was my first Christmas paycheck, and my folks were going to have a holiday we'd all remember.

I laid a new-style digital clock on the counter. My mother had no electric clock and I knew she'd never seen one like this. Next, I set a toaster down, followed by some jewelry—inexpensive, but something she'd be proud to wear on her infrequent dress-up trips away from home. My dad, an avid sportsman, would get a new fiberglass fishing rod and a tackle box. Next, some outdoor magazines—he loved to read—and one of the best pocketknives in the showcase. Other things were added up until I sensed my paycheck was about used up.

Then I topped off the pile with one final gift. It wasn't for Dad or Mom. It was for the three of us—something to remind us of those Christmases at Bah and Grandma Ora's when we had no electricity and their tree was always so exciting with those magical, colored lights. Although we now had electricity, Mom still decorated the tree with old ornaments and paper chains. Laying the largest box of colored lights I could find on the counter, I knew my normally traditional-minded mother would happily accept the change these lights symbolized.

When I finished my Christmas Eve shopping that cold winter night so many years ago, I knew four people were going to be happy—the store owner, my parents, and especially me.

The Tobacco Shop proprietor, guessing correctly what I was doing, found some gift wrap, and together we spent several delightful minutes—he adding up the bill and I wrapping the gifts.

As I carried my packages to my car, I reflected on what a great bargain I had made. Merely a week's paycheck, plus a little more, for a rather belated "homecoming" message. It would hopefully tell my parents, especially my dad, what I always found so difficult to say or show: "I love you and thanks for giving me the things that a paycheck can't buy, and for loving me as best you know how." This was really what mattered, and the fact that in the past few hours I had come to realize this.

The lights were still on when I drove up beside the house. As I carried in the presents, Mom met me in the kitchen with a startled look on her face—whether from seeing me with my arms full of gifts or from seeing me at all, I wasn't sure.

Taking some of the packages from my arms, she asked, "What's all this?"

Not waiting for a response, and unable to disguise her delight, she called, "Morris, George is home!"

My dad, sitting by the old wood-burning stove in the dining room with a blanket around his shoulders, reading, made no reply but glanced up with a somewhat surprised look as I entered the room to lay some gifts under the dark, drab-looking tree.

Thinking this night would be like any other for him and my mother, he didn't expect me home this early. But he did seem pleased in a rather quizzical sort of way when I handed him the box of colored lights to open.

"Mother, look at these," he said as he held up the box for her to see.

Her reply was merely a pleased smile as she bustled into the kitchen. "I'll fix us all a bite to eat. George, have you had any supper?"

"No. I'll eat something," I hollered over the sound of pans banging. She always was noisier in the kitchen when she was in a good mood.

As Dad and I strung the lights on the tree, I tried to make small talk. It was difficult, but I realized Dad was also trying. I didn't remember him ever helping decorate a Christmas tree, and here I was nineteen and he was doing it for the first time.

For some reason, I really didn't want to talk about my experiences of that evening in Marathon, but my father's timid attempts at conversation prompted me.

"Dad, I saw Frank tonight."

He stopped and looked at me. "Who?"

"Frank. Remember? Bah's hired man?"

"Where'd you see him?" he asked, resuming the light stringing and straightening some of the decorations that had become disarranged.

"At his son's home in Marathon. I was delivering some fuel oil."

Dad was silent for a minute and then said, "It's been a good many years . . . I don't quite remember when . . ."

"Dad, it was on Christmas Eve about ten years ago. Don't you remember that night at Bah and Grandma Ora's?" I looked at him to see if he remembered. "When he left during the night, he went home to be with his family. They hadn't seen him in years."

"The hired man! So that's why we never saw him again! To be with his family? Didn't know he had one. Never mentioned it."

As I plugged the cord in, the tree came to life. In fact, the entire room did. Suddenly it wasn't the same room; it had a warmth I had never really noticed.

As we turned to the table where Mom was setting a late-night supper, Dad repeated, "Never mentioned his family. Wonder why."

"I suppose there are many things we find hard to talk about," I answered.

As he looked across the table at me, I knew Dad wanted to say more than he finally did, but he couldn't. All he could manage to get out was "Anything else happen today, son?" I smiled as I thought of the greeting Diane's Grandpa Frank had received upon his return home ten years ago. But from my dad, that simple question was like a warm embrace.

Epilogue

THE CHRISTMAS OF 1957 WAS THE LAST Christmas my dad enjoyed sharing with his family. Sylvia and I had been married for five years, had three children, and I was back in college in my third year at the State University of New York at Cortland. Bah had passed away three years earlier, and my grandmother, unable to abide the memories associated with the home my grandfather and she had shared for well over half a century, had moved out of it and in with relatives.

My young family was now living in the home

Frank had visited on that Christmas night sixteen years earlier. That same small room at the top of the stairs where he had spent so many sad nights was still open to visitors, who never knew of the sorrowful figure who had spent rainy afternoons gazing out that window toward a home, just twelve miles to the south, filled with memories.

My father, now only thirteen months away from death with cancer, and mother would soon be moving in with us to spend Dad's last days with the grandchildren he loved. No anger or frustration was left in his life, only resignation and the simple pleasures he found, between bouts of pain, in knowing he was loved. It was late, but we still had time for father-son talks as he and Bah had had on their long summer evenings years before. We talked of Bah and Frank and hot haying weather and rainy-day fishing trips . . . and Christmas nights by the fireside. Life on Gee Hill, where we had lived these past few generations, was restrictive, but neither of us spoke of any regrets. He laughed when reminded of his torn rear pocket that my oldest son used to hang on to when learning to walk as he followed his adored grandfather about the farm.

I know Dad would have done things differently if life could be lived over; most of us would. But when he passed away in the same small bedroom where he had been born fifty-nine years earlier, my own loving family was living proof that his life had not been without purpose.

Printed in the United States
By Bookmasters